Rose Bloom Journal

Property of

____

If found,

please contact me by

Phone: ____________________

Email: ____________________

Cover Photography by Izzy Viker and Interior Design by Kevin Moyers

Printed in the United States of America

First Printing, 2020

ISBN 978-1-64852-120-1

Bunny 17 Media
Chandler, AZ, USA

www.Bunny17Media.com

CPSIA information can be obtained
at www.ICGtesting.com
Printed in the USA
LVHW010309070121
675853LV00006B/328